AFTERWARDS

Patricia Cumming

Cover by Franz S. Beer

I would like to thank the editors of the following publications
where versions of some of these poems originally appeared:

"In Reply to Letters of Condolence" and "Metaphor for Love"
reprinted with permission from *Unicorn*, volume II, no. 1,
copyright © 1970 by Karen Rockow;
"Hopewell Church" and "Return" copyright © 1969 and 1972
by *Shenandoah* reprinted from *Shenandoah:* The Washington and
Lee University Review, with permission of the Editor;
"Return" also appeared in *Best Poems of 1972*, Borestone
Mountain Poetry Awards;
"Early April" in *The Colorado Quarterly*, Autumn 1972;
"The Sea Shore" in *Let's Eat the Children*, an anthology from the
Cambridge Street Artist's Cooperative, copyright © 1972 by
Patricia Cumming;
"The Garden" in *The Little Magazine,* summer 1970;
"For Ted (1)" in *Hanging Loose* 14, May 1971;
"Notes from a Tour" and "Afterwards" in *Thursday*, copyright ©
1973 by Patricia Cumming.

ALICE JAMES BOOKS
138 Mount Auburn Street
Cambridge, Massachusetts 02138

for Edward Cumming
(1933-1960)

Though what's the use of this or any poem,
contrived small chronicle of ruin,
while Adonais rots in the red mud
of another, violent spring?

CONTENTS

1

2

3

Images

1

In that bitter country, acid as an old
photograph, there are brown
mountains, brown streets and
houses; nothing green grows, but you are
there; and I am, our daughters. Time

passes in that country, it is all
mapped; you are there, somewhere;
you don't write or
rarely, you don't come.
Ashes burn my throat.

I've learned the houses, roads, the hidden
courts and alleys, I walk
uphill, carrying
the children, to dust- and wind-
filled offices: the records that name you tear,

crumble. Then you are there,
at home, in my room, and I scream,
scream curses— You've been screwing fat
pink women, you don't answer, it is brown
in that country, nothing

grows, I have learned
it by heart, I must visit
every
night, you are there, I ransack
the dead streets.

(1969)

10

IN REPLY TO LETTERS OF CONDOLENCE

Don't praise him after he's dead.
He once could change and was not always certain.
Be as silent as though he were living.
But those who break and need sun,
praise them.

(1961)

FORBIDDING MOURNING: A MALEDICTION

Both nuns and mothers worship images,
But those the candles light are not as those
That animate a mother's reveries,
But keep a marble or a bronze repose;
And yet they too break hearts.

W. B. Yeats

I

Images! Licking at love
as to assuage it: ̗cold flickering
wisps like northern lights, but more compelling
than the world's tight walls
and disciplines; than, sometimes,
my children's panic:
                          Images!
My love's clenched like a pine knot
flare, hot
as mortality, my love has all
my reality, my love lies in a lead
coffin (to postpone decay), in a rotted coat,
wearing glasses. Have the hinges rusted
after three springs in the red
voracious dirt? Do the lenses rest
on his skull's blank holes
magnifying the darkness? What remains
of him, of his stunned, human
flesh: stench
at least? O let there be one
sense left he spins

to blazing, that cries out he changes
and exists! For what will become
of us when thou art pure
elemental bone packed
in mud? Or will that coffin keep
even the peaceful earth
out? Images
are not enough.

Those I manufacture now
keep him out of it.
They give me some rest.
But they are neither life nor death.

                    II

Last spring I had a dream
of a woman in a long black dress
with two black-barred green
birds hovering
over her shoulder.
I knew at once she was Death.
She took me to him
in a large room.
Unhesitating, I went in.
He was without any hope,
and I went out again.
But he'd smiled at me with such welcome!
And tapped, one time, to knell my going.
Love, love, O withstand!

III

This spring, in Paris, I stood at the window
of a friend's house, in tears
because of a children's song
(*"Que donneriez-vous, la belle, pour avoir vot'mari?"*
—Je donnerais mon cœur qui bat jour et nuit).
I cry hardly ever.
It was Easter morning, the first warm day,
shocking, of the year.
Light and heat and the new damp green leaves
textured the hazy air.
It was a day on which there was nothing to do
but make love.
The children laughed, discovered; lost, mourned;
and, when we went out, squeezed together
in the car,
but among the adults, behind me, in the apart-
ment, and later, in the woods,
no one touched, so much as a hand on an arm;
and yet, I think, they were as much aware
as I of that day's Promises,
as much betrayed by them, and their betrayers—

I saw him in the street. He was shining,
shining. Not with an air of vision,
he was simply as he would have been, spring
splashing on his face and arms,
coming to eat with us in that clear apartment,
bringing presents. Julie and Sue, in new
white dresses,

14

had nests of real chocolate turtles, fishes, eggs,
      and hens.
Images aren't enough!

I didn't tell anyone I'd seen him,
though perhaps they knew.
We were trying to live through that day
      in cool white prisons,
and it seemed, to me at least, like too much
sun. Also, I was trying to stop
crying for the children's sake. The children.

I spent the afternoon talking about Joy
      in a low voice.
Anyway, suffering's a luxury I can't afford.
    But had he been there we would have lain
    together in a meadow or a bed,
    hoped, atoned, conceived: invulnerable, inane,
    immortal——
            But he was dead.

IV

Mind cried, over my heart's din,
"Be content!
Spirit to spirit so bent
are blended into one
and need no bodily sustenance—
it's well known.
The green birds have gone.
Light has dispersed the shadows."

My heart said, "No.
It was I,
not you, summoned him there,
all sensory and fair—
dense: for one stride,
blotting out part of the building on the other side,
between the sidewalks,
in the street. It was I,
desire knowing nothing of Death,
who filled in the insupportable shape
of his absence:
fingers can't love air!
no matter how well they've known
the contour of nape and muscle over bone.
I should have run
to meet him on the stairs;
our kiss would not have been spiritual
but wet as these tears."

My mind persisted, "Be
still. Beware of death's
traps. Open your tight arms,
and light
will turn back the night."

My heart said, "No.
You can only dream, make images, but I,
living in spite of all,
must cry out and clamor at that line
of head and back and shoulder,
undeterred, unresigned.
There may be other lines to stir me so,
but his must wake in me
this first wild longing,
unaltered, unresigned, and unassuaged,
until I'm cinders on his grave."

V
(For Julie)

Long-legged little girl throwing a ball
in the littered suburban woods,
you guessed I cried this morning.
Mothers never cry.

Bright-haired little girl,
throwing and catching with so much concentration—
O arsenal of skill
you bravely build,
may it suffice
may it suffice
my child!
against the batteries of desolation.

VI

The children dance about my lines,
jumping thunderously from chair to floor while I
try to fix my heartbeat on this page as still
as the clay archaic smile
of an ancient votive figurine.

I remember another spring, on a hill.
He looked down at me, at moss and grass,
and I looked up, behind his head,
at arches of birches.
The leaves were small and separate, their stiff pattern,
not yet consumed by summer's avid clutter, clear
against the glittering domed sky.

The valley's gone. He found the way,
a road out of Boston, and I've forgotten.
O lost hillside! O lost Byzantine sky!
O lost *Imperator* of all my days!
Our restless children sail on unimaginable seas,
safely, in a boat of blocks, with all
            their animals and dolls:
not these—nothing!—can console
that he no longer sees, remembers,
but, in their quick splendor,
they *must* outweigh the grave.

(1962)

"He was an inspiration to us"—

I saw your shoulders there, in that space,
shrugging slightly, diffident and unaccustomed
to the glories of being the inspiriting dead,
alive with qualifications.
                                   Oh Ted!
I had forgotten for a while the long
line of your back and how warm
and rational a room
was when you were in it.
                                   Is
the only way to live
at peace in these strange places
                                   to forget?

(1962)

20

HOPEWELL CHURCH

"He was lang a-growing"
—Scottish ballad

Bare cottonstalks, ragged corn in the red clay fields.
The southern Christmas lawns are green.
Boys explore the bright pale hills,
climb and swing in the frozen, eroded ravines.
(He was long a-growing)

How simply various this farming country is
in its gentle, set winter precision,
cows, fields, fences, a few big trees
to cool the knoll-top houses summer evenings;
(He was long a-growing)

This quiet landscape which shall never be made
        famous
now—mine, at best, is a mockingbird's song,
lacks place names and the names of the trees,
the boy who taught them to me gone.
(He was long a-growing)

But the child was always gone, North to school;
he happily wandered far: I have no elegy for him.
He grew free here, as he wanted to,
remembered where the brooks ran when he
        came home.
(He was long a-growing)

Long ago, this was remote country, and the fields,
golden still, of his great-grandfathers' farms—

>   *Enough of landscape!*
>   *It's just this strip of it*
>   *I must bring myself to consider—*

now reaped only in the great aunt's stories, are
            sold,
vanish: under the power lake's muddy, insatiable
            arms.
>   *(He was long a-growing)*

>   *This plot.*

>   Two towhees hop, doomed, busy and tranquil
>   on the brilliant grass (passionate
>   about fact, he taught me their names),
>   and a grey squirrel jumps, more alert
>   to catastrophe—

This space which surely is too short for him!

>   *(He was long a-growing)*

(I've only been here twice before
since it hid irreparably any part,
ring or bone to which I was wedded
in a summer garden:
once when the broken red dirt

clotted my dazed heart,
and once at midnight
with a warm wind in the old trees,
when we—his brother and I—could see
            nothing;

The first time, terrified and unprepared,
I found and burned some of his tobacco;
the second time we came with Nuits-St.-Georges,
and drank till we were drunk and half in love,
not forgetting our libation to the earth,
but those were times I thought some ceremony,
necessarily secret in this strict, pious place,
might unite, assuage, or continue us; celebrate,
raise or settle his ghost, I hardly know which—
what is ceremony supposed to do?—
and before I saw how the grass
had implacably matted over his coffin.)

            This plot.

As close as I shall ever come to him again,
six inches of frozen consecrated ground,
and my fingers grapple with the magic letters
            of his name
on the cold pale stone,
and beat aimlessly at the rough, indecipherable
            grass
scattered with acorns. No ceremony
can dissolve this earth between us. No ceremony

can comfort me or him, frozen
as we are until the terrible spring
mud shall erupt and spawn
in our entrails, leaving
me, unprepared as always,
to break my racing heart on visions
in the wind. No ceremony's any use.
The grass long growing.

And yet this ground contains
such Treasure, such inordinate desire—
all the rough and fine
shapes and particles of earth caught
in his nerves like the jewels
of buried kings—as should quake
the dull church bricks where they buried him
(with quick assurances of some
airy immortality beyond the racing rings
of blood), and crack
the foundations of the sun
with the faceted exactness of his love!

O metaphor: Pathetic
fallacy: Make me now a ceremony
who needs it just as much as always
for the speechless blank event of Ted's dying,

for these defeated tears—
turn them into stars!
Find at least some resolution,
for this ordinary, golden, cold afternoon,
hard as rock,
for otherwise I am still helpless,
I am still helpless on this small flat grave.

(New Year's Day, 1963)

RETURN

Well, I've come back to the place where your
                 bones are,
bringing your children, pigtailed, almost reading.
My eyes ache.
You would think, you would think
after five years..... But the reddish clay
is still like blood.
                We have Christmas together,
your family and I. They do not speak of you,
as if I were here for some other reason——

     I cower in the vaulted
     silence, but the stabbing light might——

yet they must grieve in their way.
They grieve. Each ornament on the tree
is their memory, for the children.

     But there are too many of them,
     all these people who are not
     you, but have your hair, your eyes,
     your speech, energy, some of your ways;
     the arched sky crashes, splinters
     as if into stars
     to celebrate a child's
     birth here——

But, in the dark, the cut tree looms, its
electric eyes transfix me, and its gaudy
claws surround, clutch. I say,
"How lovely!" lying (our daughters watch),
sleep, sleep. The Yule tides rise.

> *I drown, my fists full*
> *of wet stones.*

(1965)

EARLY APRIL

The children can't sleep either. Spring comes
fitfully by day, but the nights
falter, the promise broken. Grey
snow nests in the corners of the garden and today
I saw a black, tailless cat eating the sooty crocuses.
Two grown clerks from the Stop & Shop played,
in the sun, merciless and unjoyous, hide and seek
around a trailer truck. No wonder

the world hesitates to be born again.
My husband's bones
sift in the mud. He loved. We
who have lived bleed
on the fences of our choices, our unchosen
givens. I look for words

dense enough to catch our shifting visions,
but find instead
my daughters cramped in nightmare, this
amputated cat, and those two clean-cut
sterile men ambushing each other
          on Hancock Street.
To have said one thing clearly

could have been a reason to endure.

(1965)

28

2

FOR SAMMY: IN PRAISE

I

Sammy, who had lived with us for years,
brought the cat, Pierre,
back to my mother in New York,
before she went to the hospital
to die of cancer.
She had taken him to her house in the country,
but its apparent peace had proved
at length bewildering to his aged,
ravenous senses; he was lost three days.

The old man,
my step-father, who had once ignored him,
now finds common cause with this cat,
almost blind, stumbling.
It's the same cat: I remember
him, young, from my childhood house,
where no one   ever   died.

                    Sammy
dreamed as fiercely as any of us
who lived there, above a river
which ebbed and grew with the tide;
her gifts lay
in the mortal arts, splendid irregular bouquets
of flowers, and food. Idiomatic,
exact, she made my tautened mother
almost relax, allayed
pretend catastrophes. Thin,
scared, lonely as I was then, battered by half-seen
reflected shadows in familiar rooms,
into what wild place might I have come
had not Sammy taken me in
as one of her own? Her love raged,
rampant as lions, on the wide sunny planks
of the polished floors of that house.

                    Later, in New York,
Sammy married, but, after her second operation
          for cancer,
off and on, her husband left her.
My parents were divorced.
"What can you *do?*" she said. She remade,
cooked, straightened: fierce,

critical, protective, she built her perishing bouquets
larger, larger. In the big house
where my mother came to live with my step-father
she made desserts with dozens of eggs.
"Oh Patsy! I used a pint of sherry! It was a
         situation!"
She bought a house, adopted
a son; I married; everything seemed at last
settled; but the dust she'd shifted,
cleaned out of crannies in so many houses, rose
         in clouds
against her: she fought
it back. When my first child
was born she came down South
and taught me how to cook okra, and turnips
         with sour cream.
She saw to it
the baby had a bathinette I didn't want.
After my husband died she begged me not
         to wear black.

                              Now,
always small, she is at last
thin. Too thin, she's lost thirty pounds!
I didn't recognize her
in the dim apartment lobby, the bleak glare
of the city street blazing behind her.
She brought the cat and her last
gift, a pot of parsley for my mother.
When I put my arms around her,
where there was always warmth,
I felt her bones.

My step-father puts on his white cap,
tilts it, and starts for New York.
We see him fumbling with the lock
and pull him back. He's too frail
to resist us now; he can hardly speak.
Busy, cowards, we do not even hope
that, in the wide blank street,
sense, amazed, would quicken to an avid blaze
of vision, strength: we guard instead
against calamity, and will not see
where that will lead us, either—
mortal as he, and as uncertain at the clanging
          doors,
as bewildered by the shifting
changeful buttons in the elevator
rocketing to foreign floors,
until Odysseus stumbles home,
asking for bed, forgiveness. My mother
does not generalize. Panic
scalds her harrowing reproaches. She forgets;
and promises them both a life when he is well.
"I get so tired now," she says.
When she can leave him she takes the train
to Grasslands Hospital, in Valhalla,*
where Sammy is.
The women talk about the past.

---

* In order to be admitted she had to sign her house
over to the hospital, as security against the eventual
bill.

III

The cat got fat again. I moved to Boston.
But I came back, and went out to the hospital
Thanksgiving Day. Sammy
had a tube down her throat
so she could breathe, and a pad
of lined yellow paper. She wrote,
the pad turned sideways, in pencil, across the
                lines,
"Patsy im glad you came you no i wont get well."
I had been told. I didn't know.
Did she? Did she? She looked so small,
lying there in the great waves of the bed,
like a child, only greater. There were photographs
of all of us taped to the walls;
there was no future.
Does she know how my love calls
from the eyes of the still child,
the stiff bride?—When I went out of her room
it was clear wide sunset, gold air
I breathed for the first time,
o splendor! splendor! When I left
she was so tired, crumpled,
that breath,
the loss of the day's sun,
would have been too hard for her,
but other days she must have known,
alone, the damp leaves, the sky
she left behind.

IV

Hollowness.
Starched, in white, the guardians
put the cat out of his misery.
My step-father lives
in a hospital now, on a hill.
Mother thinks he will come home.

Hollowness. The hospital's
apparent calm, my quietness (Sammy,
if I am still, very still,
will you rest, will you
stay?).
       Now Sammy has died.

V

       Remember.
She remembered: what we loved and suffered.
Out of it, the fear,
the promises, the bitterness rampant down the
       corridors of blood,
out of truth and her dream,
she made
       a basilica, ancient, glimmering,
and left it for us to recognize
if we can
       when the shadow passes: Sammy,
a wraith at the end in the huge white bed,
surrounded by mute oblongs that were us,
remembered,
       and made it whole.

Note

Sammy was a Negro (her word). I did not put this in the poem because I did not want it to be about "race". Writing today (1970), I would have had to say she was Black. She wasn't. She was brown, changing as light under trees.

But this is a poem about race nevertheless. I knew her only because she was Black, and poor. She did not finish school, but had she done so, and gone on to occupy the position to which her intelligence, her ability with people and with language, her standards and her concern entitled her, she would not have taken care of me.

I wanted to pretend there was no difference between us; I wanted to be like her, either, or any, color (I still do). But there was a difference — even as a child I knew she was not respected as she should have been; I was hurt, puzzled by this, angry. Now I know there is more to what life was like for her, fear. She did not tell me. What she showed was what she made from it, courage.

I did not go to her funeral, because then I would have had to *know* that we were separate; I would have gone, inevitably, with my mother — a white lady, an alien; and it seemed to me that the courtesy and welcome of her real family would have only made the distance greater. But in fact I had been able to maintain the fiction that race was not important only because at times she consented to live in my world, no matter what it cost her. She came to my wedding, the only brown person there; and I should have gone to her funeral, and worn gloves, and a hat, as she would have wished.

I wanted to say differences do not matter (and so avoid a number of painful facts, among them, her suffering), but it is not true. They made part of her life, and mine; and had I seen, remembered, then what was different could not, even at the end, have separated us.

NOTES FROM A TOUR

Like most
educated Americans I have my hard won
culture, I've been to Vézéley
at dusk, dined at Lapérouse,
sat
on the gold stone blocks of the Acropolis,
and I have this to tell you:
the dead are not still and the living
freeze.

Even my father,
whose bulk was muscle, suffocated
fury—his ashes, where
are they (Did
she
charter a plane and scatter them
as she said she would,
or does she keep them in a
jar

in her drawer?
She does not sleep in their old room,
offered it to the children:
I took it. Now he's
dead
I can sleep alive in my Daddy's bed, dive deep—
I slept well, too, did not
dream: but his ashes,
where

                    are they?)
shifting in what waters or uneasy
     in an "urn"?
     Yes, he
                    cries
out as he did before he died,
     and my husband, now
     earth, grass, trees,
               bleeds

          under the pious
mower and the storm's crack—
     I know, I
     have sharp ears
               nights
when the children are asleep and all's
     swirling. The monuments
     are incised with the chiseled signs of dead
               men;

          those who
live, eat as they can, struggle to
     build, not quite open, or kind: from
     inward a cry, stilled, cuts their
               faces,
constricting them. We must remember
     this, I tell you, nights
     when our only friends are our
               ghosts,

          free
of the stone cast of living.

THE SEA SHORE

For my father

I

The bright
sky glittering
glittering   green
as slime — o what's

this landscape?
The sand blazes
white as
death, the horizon's

scarred, huge deaf
stone figures gnaw
it and the air burns
out breath like a child's

jarring
loneliness: her
furnaces shiver in the hot
air —

o come and be
killed, killed, killing!
o the small grey birds
circle and *kaah!*

II

Grown, I was also
afraid
on the way to
the crematorium where

they burned
my deaf fat
father's big
body up. He was dead

already, I could not have stopped
that, but I might have
frozen, halted
the procession, turned

off my headlights, stopped and sat
hunched, black, and dusty there by the thun-
            dering thru-
way, and wept.
That was years ago, but the light

blinds me still, and the lucid
green water washes, washes
on the sand, whispering, o come,
come, I will put all fires

out.

THE GARDEN

The door to this garden seems to be
half open—my room's bare,
cold—I can't
go through it. Alone?

The country house was devoured
by fire; the tall dark
woods danced; Aba, the gentle
burned cook, screamed; the child

was cold, blue as fear, for-
gotten. *Mama!* But she ran
away to save the silver.
It melted. *I will forget*

Aba's face as she has lost mine
in her dead darkness. The garden?
Mine? The sun's like the reflections
of fire on the shrubbery.

Later, the centaur stood in it,
laughing, one hoof curled
under him, then
he galloped away, and I pressed

my nose against the window,
watching. What windy
spaces out there, what deceptive
hollows, and then—

cliffs! I know how it is
to stutter at the edge
of the darkness, cracked
(my heart's flimsy!); oh, yes,

it's cold. Watch
the ravens, they
aren't appeased, one reddish wire
claw can dislodge me, one dried grass nest can

rot in the sandstone
fissures and crevasses—
the seed roots, pierces,
drives me into darkness—

*you who have not
known danger, listen*
to me: you may be left
with photographs, flowerpots,

records, letters, the heat's
like a house burning, but this
lightning splinters
into Arctic oceans, I can only

pretend it does not. Lie
to live. *Dear Mama.* This seeming
room! HA HA ha ha ha . .
. . .

Oh, it's strange. I teach
my children all the tables,
doors, the radiator—
who's crazy? Well, I tell you,

if we work very hard
we'll make it coherent, type it
up, argue
out our complicity. Reason's

our weapon—standard!
Hooray! But let us not
presume. Mud's crawled
out of slimy seas, and we

are hardened waste
products of evolution,
camping in Boston,
with a soot-stained yard.

There's no other:
garden. Rise
out of nightmare; twice
a year, put

ground white limestone on it: myrtle
and pachysandra may grow.

THE GARDEN (2)

The country house was devoured
by fire; the tall dark
trees danced; the child was cold,
blue with fear. *Aba!* But she ran

away into the house,
into her room to save
something. She melted.
I will forget

Aba's face as she has lost
mine in her dead
darkness. A garden?
Mine? The sun's like the reflections—

I did not—
It did not happen.

I did not cry.

They said she was resting,
in the country.

She is in a garden.

A dark garden.

There was a child who dropped
matches in the furnace pipe.
It exploded.
That was a bad child.

If they find out they will kill her.

I will hide her.

I will kill her.

They whispered, Aba,
Aba is

Maybe she—

I've forgotten. Even a word—

I make a country out of air.
Where voices—

In this country they do not speak to me.
A word—

But I keep her, for-
getting! Dark, light. A word—

Her voice turned
thin as the air.
I would like to remember it now,
I can't, I—

   That other
   that other garden
   dark!
   even dark   she is there

It is all blinding
as the flames, as her scream.
Behind them, dimly,
at the end of a hall

she speaks so gently
I can not
understand. I look
through dusty boxes of the terrible

past, I find only faded brown
negatives; but one comes
out clearly. She was
very young, strong, and a baby

played near her, in a stream, with stones.
We were in a garden.

GARDENS

                     A green
landscape. Leaves blow
in the wind, pale underneath.
Behind the wind is

absence, beyond the trees,
a rock country, airless.
I can not breathe.
I waited

through another winter, did not
hope, I waited to come back
to the summer, to gardens,
fields: they said

she was in the country, but she was not
here still, not in my
country; she left without a
word, there was no message

in the leaves though they spoke her
name, *Elizabeth, Elizabeth,*
formally, as
at her marriage or her birth.

Where is
she? I have looked in other
landscapes, other climates where
rosemary, lemons

grow; I have kept
looking, in the mountains,
by the ocean, stretching to see
over hedges, through gates, behind

walls: all my life I've believed
the children's
books, where at the end who is gone
comes, comes:

the fear, the waiting are
over, and you can
cry— If you wait
long enough.

But now my life has
crumbled, it sifts
through my hands, dust
speckled with mica, twigs,

leaves from another
season, and the dry wind
blows. Behind the wind is death.
Death lurks in the sea, it holds out

wet hands. I waited.
But the gardens
are flat, there, simply,
and I have almost forgotten

who I am looking
for, except that I am frightened and
mourn, when spring
comes. They told me

and I know
now she is dead, she burned
up she flamed she screamed
she melted, and the books

are wrong: they do not tell
you how to cry or that life
stretches out, day after day;
and that the gardens,

even the ones by the sea with roses
and marigolds in them,
are always
empty.

GRAVEYARDS

I

Where
are the dead, where
among the tall wild grasses?
—At the roots a forestful
of insects, and the tops
are
heavy with seed and wind.
The old stones
are mossy, rain blown, worn,
and time
passes, and has been.

II

New Yorkers
mourn their myriad
dead here, in granite vaults
or plots—care guaranteed
for a hundred
years.
The grass is fertilized technicolor green,
each faulty limb of shrub
or tree is lopped, decay has been
stopped,
there's no reawakening.

III

Here
are   flags,   faded
wax flowers, ribbons under glass;
and here, on *la día de los muertos,*
families, dogs, children,
come,
bringing sugar skulls, toys, picnics;
they gossip among the grave
stones, and every morning the dawn
wind
blows the tattered crepe to banners again.

IV

I wish
my husband had been buried
in a mountain graveyard or in a forest
as he wanted; here, he's clenched, stiff,
twisted, and my mind bats
at his still light
like a moth: for until the place speaks
of him truly — silencing their
prayers, damning, fattened on his
corpse,
lying — he cannot change, become

spring
by dying, dying
and I can't leave him to the rain,
wind, stone, the tall grasses
blowing.

3

Metaphor for Love

A young bird follows autumn winds
and flies, although it cannot see enough
to know if ever the ocean stops
or if this passionate journey south
is only journeying to death:
but sure that turning off
leads to a denser darkness, a more piercing frost.

For Ted

1.

Now you swing, dead my
dear, on the gargoyles and
frets of the cathedral
spires, but the stuffed
heads in my room—lions—
hydras—hummingbirds—zebras —
smell of formaldehyde.

2.

Rats in his classroom, he
kneels in the wilderness, and I hear
him clatter—shut
up, the racket!   You were warm
once, no one

bothers.   Except that I
sleep, sleep, dropping
too far (where Pluto the father
of the irreconcilable dead   watches us,
aimless):   time

gnaws, and it's not far off,
where you are.

3.

"In Brazil, you know,
even owls play. Forget
the dead, climb in the plain
trees," the wise—
they call themselves wise—
men say.

4.

The walls rattle
with emptiness. Cats
stare from corners
and walk (step
paw, step paw) across
my desk. You
whom I love I
hate. You are in no way anything but
good, but
gone. Your warmth's
gone, your eyes,
voice. Your death consumed it,
the old cities, the gardens, the rooms:
you have fed me
to the winds, love;
rancor cuts
my throat; and the cats' yellow
eyes watch my vanishing
face.

Song

I was all closed, contained,
quiet: widowed but almost
resigned (I had my house, job,
children), a bit
lonely (but no one, not
even I, knew how much):

now, for a voice, a face,
I walk, possessed, in the winter
rain, aching, skewered by dreams,
open, open to the winds—

and all, all for nothing.

Query

My mouth is full of
cuts. My breath smells like
rust. As
in a dream the dentist scrapes

my teeth, disinfects
them with peroxide. How
can I love   anyone, be
loved, tasting

rot?

On Self-Deception

He must be odd
as a Romanesque
capital, hard,
rational and tense
as mathematics, wild
as Pan: I do not need

to love
an ordinary living man.

Second Song

I'm not in love, I'm still
as a cedar twisted long ago
by storms, now closed in a young field,
its flaky
trunk lapped by buttercups.
The fine thin needles curl flat,
calm; and the branches lift gently,
stiffly—no longer wrenched
awry, breaking
in hurricanes of a voice or bent by the steady
sea winds of dream. It's noon, hot,
silent.
      Yesterday
I loved him, and tonight   under the moon
the wind will rise.

Dream

He who had fallen
                    came
back: His speech was altered,
colder; we lay like cobwebs

on the long beds. I am afraid
of him, of my love, I cannot speak
to this stranger
                    after his silence.

Second Dream

I shake myself after
love, brush
my hair, and wrap
up in an old
old Brooks Brothers bathrobe—
we were, after all, only
naked, but he had a spiky
beard like a Renaissance
Prince, and a gaiety in his eyes
that reminded me love
of you.

Third Song

Sometimes I love him
and sometimes I do not,
but in the moments I love   the leaves
have edges like knives,
and beyond the tall grass rustling in my field
I can hear the mower   rasp.

Drawing Lesson

Half an inch
high, you stand (cheerfully,
alive), a long
way away

in the upper left
corner of the picture.
I can barely
see your face. But the roads,

the rivers all run
to you, the trees, the horizon
point to you, the sun the sky
shines on you: I

am learning perspective.

This Journey

Who am I? changed
because of him,
because of his hands?

We walked in summer
fields. Wind
blew at the Queen Anne's lace.
Waves splashed on the rocks
and we gathered
mussels at low tide.
We didn't talk much.

Perhaps we were afraid.

But the sun shone and at night
we could see the whole sky.

We seemed to hold time still.

I have no words.
They go in and out of my mind,
they blow away and fall like leaves
in the woods, fall on moss,
ferns, and ground pine.

Who is he? I watch
as much as I dare,
as I can,
but my eyes are too full of him
to see; I only know his name;
I breathe his air.

AFTERWARDS

And when they left it, did Eden
remain? Isolated, perfect, each
leaf without holes, as in a painting
by Cranach, or Rousseau? Is it there

still, in Iraq, India, or Tanzania, where
too many generations (their pasts interlocked,
rooted, holding them) have fought
for its earth worked to

desert: and starve? Does it
exist, that first, completed
place, there and not
there, in other, disjoint

dimensions—and if you learned
the equation or could recognize
the amarynth,
could you then pierce

those perfect spheres
of air,
and enter there,
where nothing has changed?

But I think that stillness must
have vanished when the eyes
of those who loved it turned away
to wilder

worlds: the adamantine walls
crumbled, under vines, brambles,
seasons, and the pollinating, leaf-
devouring insects blew

in. And then—even those composed first
plants grew tangled
roots, stretched, branched, and inter-
locked for a share of air

and earth, forcing change,
forcing rot, and forcing
life in that frozen perfect country
only for the dead.